THE RISING GENERATION: No-Pit-4-Us

EUNICE R. CALLWOOD

THE RISING GENERATION : NO - PIT - 4 - US

Eunice R. Callwood
email: e_callwood@yahoo.com

ISBN: 978-1-949826-15-9
Printed in the USA.
All rights reserved

Published by: EAGLES GLOBAL Publishing | Frisco, Texas
In conjunction with the 2019 Eagles Authors Course
Cover & interior designed by PublishAffordably.com | (773) 783-2981

PRESENTED

To:

_____

From:

_____

Date:

_____

Event:

_____

DEDICATION

This book is dedicated to my grandchildren, and godchildren, their children, and the generations to come.

Children of my nieces, nephews, cousins, and friends.

Teenagers within my church community.

Teenagers within my immediate
residential and social community.

Teenagers residing in the territories
of the United States Virgin Islands.

Teenagers living in the British Virgin Islands.
Teenagers throughout the Caribbean Islands.

Teenagers across the United States.
Teenagers around the world.

Teens, you were born with a purpose and destined for greatness. You are equipped with skills and talents that will benefit you, your family, and your community. This manuscript is a "life guide," and it is designed to help you achieve your dreams and fulfill your purposes without the burdens of pitfalls.

The consequences of pitfalls can make living quite daunting. So, grab some friends, select your favorite snacks, put your feet up, and get ready to indulge in the exciting pages of this book - The Rising Generation: No - Pit - 4 - Us!

ACKNOWLEDGMENTS

First, I give honor to my Lord and Savior, Jesus Christ, for in Him, I live and move and have my being. Thank you for allowing this life guide to be written in this season, and thanks for giving me the opportunity to be a part of impacting this generation in a positive and meaningful way. You called the young because they are strong, and I am humbled to take this journey with them. Thank you, Abba Father.

To my husband, Charles, who supported me along the way. He always listened and echoed his sentiments when I got excited and read certain portions of the book to him. I love you, my love!

To my daughters, Geminie and Genisa, thanks for offering your unwavering support and for making invaluable contributions to this "life guide." I love you more than you can imagine.

May my parents, Alfred Aenias and Idalia Leonard, continue to rest in peace, knowing that the good things that they have instilled in me are continuing to blossom in my life. Never-ending love!

To my siblings, Carvell Robinson, Phyllis Leonard, Ione Little, Courtney Leonard, Vincent Vanterpool, and Alfred Leonard, who have always prayed for me. Thanks for being there! I love you all.

To my church family, Faith Christian Fellowship Church Alive in Christ—thanks for the impartation of the Word of God in my life; and thanks for your love, support, and prayers.

To Pastors Fernando and Gail Leonard—your passion for the Godly development of children has been an inspiration to me. Thank you and may God bless you richly. Much love!

To my childhood church family, Apostolic Faith Mission, thanks for planting the seed of the Word of God in my life. It is this foundation that has molded me into who I am today.

To my friend, minister, psalmist, songwriter and author, Judy Turnbull, who has always stated, "Write, Eunice, write; the Lord has placed much in you." Thanks for giving me the opportunity to share at the annual ASAPH (Always Sanctified, Always, Praising, Him) youth worship conference. It was during a youth workshop that this life guide was conceived. Love you, girl! Friends forever!

To my friend Dr. Greta Hart-Hyndman, heartfelt appreciation to you for your tremendous support. Your constructive input meant the world to me. Love you much! Friends never ending!

To my friends, Prophet Levi and Monique Farrell, your prayers always reached heaven on my behalf. Thanks for standing in the gap and being a part of my life. I appreciate and love you both.

To my friends Jerry and Sheri Meyers, you both are amazing when it comes to pushing me to be my best. Thanks for your prayers and encouragement. I love you both.

To Apostle and Principal Sandra Reed, thanks for your time and dedication in providing feedback. Your input was truly valued. Much love and appreciation to you!

To my ASAPH and FCFCAIC praise team family, thanks for understanding that when I took a break from the ministry, I was fulfilling another Kingdom assignment—writing! I love you all! May God bless you!

To my friends Kelson Thomas and Margarita Benjamin, thanks for your unwavering and professional support during the entire process. I love you both, and God bless.

To my friends and prayer partners—Donna Phillips, Donna Walters, Florencia Stevens, Lavern Francis, and Veronica Richardson, thanks for remaining prayerful. The fervent prayer of the righteous avails much!

To the Eagles International Training Institute, thanks for creating this platform where authors can develop and produce their product to impact the world. God bless you for being positioned for the apostolic ministry.

EUNICE R. CALLWOOD

PREFACE

In today's society, most individuals are hooked on social media, cell phones, and technology. People spend a vast majority of their day surfing the web, watching YouTube videos, or scrolling through Snapchat, Facebook, and Instagram. There is no doubt that both technology and social media have the world's attention. It also goes without question that technology is one of the greatest advancements in the world.

But wait! What about the attention on this generation? Yes, it is you, I am talking about. You are destined to be tomorrow's parents, pastors, teachers, counselors, engineers, doctors, attorneys, plumbers, electricians, contractors, governors, and much more. The ingredients needed to keep up with social media and technology—focus, commitment, passion, energy, skills, and time—are even more needed to ensure that you become one of the next leaders without the consequences of pitfalls.

Because you and your peers are next in line to run society, it has become my passion to share the resources, experiences, insight, and knowledge that I have gained over the course of my life's journey. In so doing, I hope that you will embrace the love poured onto the pages of this book and allow the message to make a positive impact in your life. This book is designed to help you navigate through this process called life. The wisdom and guidance contained on these pages are an invaluable investment, just for you!

According to the Oxford Dictionary, a pitfall is a "hidden or unsuspected danger or difficulty."[1] Hazards, death traps, entanglements, risks, stumbling blocks, and drawbacks are all descriptions of pitfalls. Gosh! Pitfalls are heavy stuff, and they can wear you out if you have to carry their penalties throughout your life.

The Rising Generation: No - Pit - 4 - Us intends to assist you and your peers to dodge the headaches, heartaches, frustrations, and regrets that come along with these entanglements. Life does not promise that everything will go smoothly, but decreasing the likelihood of unnecessary and preventable pitfalls is key.

Recently, I was reading about "Internet challenges," and I realized that people are challenging each other to do some strange and even sometimes life-threatening stuff. For example, the Kylie Jenner lip challenge, the cinnamon challenge, and the choking/fainting/pass-out challenge went viral, drawing not only the attention but also the participation of viewers everywhere. It's incredible how we can be easily dragged into doing things that are risky! But, hey! I am here to offer you a different type of challenge. This challenge is safe, healthy, positive, pro-life, and pro-success. This challenge has your back. Yep! That's it! "The No - Pit - 4 - Us" Challenge!

This short but profound life guide will address tools and applications to steer you clear of the things and situations that can cause you to get in trouble. I hope that your focus, time, passion, and dedication will be channeled and used to your overall benefit. You will be challenged, and in turn, you can challenge your peers to dodge those snags and setbacks as you work towards good success in your lives.

So whether you are on the bus, at the park, sitting on your front doorstep, or with a group of friends, I encourage you to read through all of my messages page by page.

Do not delete, but do hit "save";
refresh when needed, and kindly share
The Rising Generation:
No - Pit - 4 - Us with your peers.

Eunice R. Callwood

CONTENTS

INTRODUCTION

Everyone, regardless of age or nationality, whether they are rich or poor, healthy or ill, educated or uneducated, can all attest to the fact that every day of their lives, they are faced with situations that require a decision. "What am I going to do? Where should I go?" Some decisions are easy to make, and others can be quite difficult. Some decisions are influenced by others, while some are not. Some decisions are risky, while others are not so risky. You may ask yourself, "Should I go to school today, or should I stay at home?" "Should I eat eggs and toast for breakfast, or should I eat a bag of chips?" "Should I fill out this college application now, or should I wait until next month?" "Should I agree to drink alcohol with my buddy, or should I say no?"

As a young person, you are bombarded by many influences and questions. Peer pressures are weighing you down. You want to fit in, decisions are not easy, and life is throwing punches at you. You wonder, "Can I get through this?" The good news is, yes you can, and help is available, so stay tuned! Once you are aware and educated on the matter and you create a good foundation on which to make your decisions, then you are on the right track. The information contained in this book will highlight some important things that you need to know and consider to make healthy lifelong decisions.

Here is a good example. Fried foods taste really good, especially when they are fried nice and crispy! But guess what? Eating large amounts of fried foods every day can increase your blood cholesterol level. Eventually, high cholesterol can cause a heart attack and/or stroke. If you decide that you do not want to have these problems, then you will avoid eating lots of fried foods, right? Did you say yes? Awesome!

Once you are aware that something is risky and can cause harm to you, then that information can help you to make the best decision to prevent pitfalls in your life. Talk about self-empowerment and self-regulation—you got this! I am rooting for you. You can and will make healthy decisions.

The third president of the United States, Thomas Jefferson, often said, "Knowledge is Power." Gaining as much knowledge as possible and using it to your advantage is certainly the path you are encouraged to take.

I am excited to share with you strategies that you can use throughout your development. I don't think that you would go through frustrations, stress, aggravation, regret, anger, setbacks, and all those negative feelings and situations if you could do something to avoid them.

Not too long ago, I was your age, and I did some dumb stuff. Fortunately for me, I was able to learn from my mistakes. Learning from my boo-boos allowed me to grow wiser and smarter throughout my experiences. The cool thing about wisdom is that, once you possess it, you can unlock some of life's richest secrets. Would you like to know one of the secrets that I discovered through gaining wisdom? Come closer, pay attention. You don't have to make your own mistakes to learn from them. How amazing is that?

Although having your own experiences in life is invaluable to your own personal growth, it's comforting to know that there are some mistakes that others have made for you, so their errors will help you avoid the consequences that they had to endure or have to live with. When a mistake happens, we can learn from it, and we are then able to share our experiences with others, which is what I'm doing with this book.

> "It's said that a wise person learns from his mistakes.
> A wiser person learns from others' mistakes.
> But the wisest person of all learns from others' successes."

> – John C. Maxwell

EUNICE R. CALLWOOD

CHAPTER ONE

THE COMPANY OF GOOD SUCCESS: THEY'VE GOT YOUR BACK

I am so happy that you decided to read this book—whether you stumbled on it in the bookstore or you were researching the topic of pitfalls. Your teacher might have selected it as a reading assignment, or your youth organization might have asked you to read it for a group discussion. Maybe a special friend or family member gave it to you as a gift, or you found it on Amazon while shopping for a special event. Regardless of how you acquired this life guide, I believe that you will not regret reading it to the end.

When you hear the word "company," what comes to mind? Primarily, I think about people and chores. Whenever I tell my family that we will be having company over for dinner or that company will be spending time with us, they automatically know that we will have to prepare. Grocery shopping, prepping meals, and tidying up the house are all ways in which we get ready for visitors. "Let's get it together, guys! We are having company over!"

A company can be a business that sells items such as clothes, shoes, or food. But it can also be defined as a group of people coming together, usually for the same purpose.

In *The Rising Generation: No - Pit - 4 - Us*, we will focus on the gathering of a group of people, not the operation of a business. There are different types of people that come together, and they have different functions, purposes, and ways of operating. I classify these groups as A) company of family, B) company of friends, and C) extended company.

A. Company of Family

Our company of family is not chosen. It is a natural occurrence. Parents (biological, adopted, foster), brothers, sisters, grandmas, grandpas, aunties, uncles, and cousins—these are your company of family. Have you heard the phrase, "Blood is thicker than water?" Well, it's an old saying that means family is more loyal to each other than to anyone else. The loyal family is dependable and supportive. These are the people that carry you deep in their hearts; it's like having the same blood running through your veins. I see the company of family as people who will do everything in their power to make sure that you do well. They will go the extra mile to protect you and ensure that you become successful.

Unfortunately, as we know, not all families function in the way God intends. There are families that, due to life's circumstances, are hurt, broken, and lack the love and support that all family units not only deserve but innately desire. Here's the thing: God in heaven sees all, and He knows all. He only requires you to do your part—love, honor, respect, pray for your family, and leave the rest to Him. All you can do is your part, and when necessary, reach out for assistance to the other companies that I will explain further as you continue to read.

B. Company of Friends

The second company is the company of friends. This company you can select—you actually have a choice with this one. A friend is loyal and supportive. A friend is someone who loves you and is forgiving. A friend has a close relationship with you. You do things together, and you have fun together. A friend is happy when you do well. Friends look out for each other, and they want the best for each other. Friends are not jealous or envious of each other. Friends correct you when you are wrong and applaud you when you are right. True friendship lasts a lifetime. The Bible states that a friend sticks closer to you than a brother.

C. Extended Company

The third company is your extended company. These are people in society who have your best interest at heart. They have a specific calling in your life. They also have a special role to play in society. These people are experts in their field of work, and they are equipped to teach, guide, support, and mentor youths. Pastors, youth leaders, principals, teachers, counselors, social workers, doctors, nurses, librarians, coaches, and psychologists are all part of your extended company.

Your company of family, your company of friends, and your extended company all have one thing in common: they want good success for you. To make it simple in your journey through this book, we will refer to these three companies as your "company of good success."

D. Good Success!

One day after reading Joshua 1:8, my eyes were stuck on the words "good success." The verse states that if we read, say, meditate on, and do what God's Word states, then our way shall be prosperous, and we will have good success.

Now, if God talks about "good success," then there must also be "bad success." You may ask, "How can that be?" Well, here is an example. Two students took a test, and both of them got a grade of 100%. Hooray! All correct! That is success! Would you agree? But let's look at how the success was earned.

The first student studied hard for many hours. He even fell asleep with the book in his hand. The other student cheated by stealing the answer sheet from the teacher's desk. The difference between good and bad success is how the success was achieved. Strive to acquire success in the right way, because bad success will not add any value to your character. Bad success will not speak well of you; bad success will give you a bad reputation. Clearly, "bad success" is gained through cheating, lying, stealing, and all other forms of corruption.

The Rising Generation: No - Pit - 4 - Us was written with you in mind. You are part of the generation that is bombarded with issues, distractions, and challenges, but the good news is that you are not alone, and there are support systems to assist you along your journey. You have quite a pool of resources to pull from to assist you in avoiding the pitfalls of life. It is in your best interest to surround yourself with family, friends, and people in your community who are a representation of good success.

Of course, no one is perfect, but the company of good success strives to do the right thing, and their reputation is good. They discourage wrong and will tell you when you are wrong. They praise and nurture good conduct and wholeheartedly provide assistance to improve negative behaviors. They have your back and want nothing less than the best for you. I am happy to be included in your company of "good success," and I do hope that you are still as excited as I am to continue our journey through these pages. We are on a mission to discover ways to conquer all that life throws at us, but before we move on, I have an activity for you to do.

No - Pit - 4 - Us

ACTIVITY 1

This is a simple activity about friendship. After reading the section on the company of friends, answer the following questions about the people you call "friends" and see how you do.

1. Is your friend trustworthy or loyal?

2. Is your friend supportive?

3. Do you and your friend do things together like shopping, homework, or going to the movies?

4. Does your family know your friend?

5. Does your friend look out for you?

6. Does your friend desire the best for you?

7. Is your friend happy when you do well?

8. Does your friend correct you when you are doing wrong?

If you answered yes to all of the questions and your friend answered yes to the questions as well, then you are doing pretty well. Congratulations!

However, it is very important to note that friendship is a relationship that takes time to grow and develop. Answering "yes" to all eight questions is great, but the most important thing is to recognize that when the answers change to "no," the friendship may be having an issue. It is super important to identify the problem, have an open conversation, and use your support systems, such as your company of good success, to assist in sorting out the problem.

CHAPTER TWO

RISING AGAINST THE PITFALLS OF LIFE

A. In Pursuit of Good Success

Teens are being influenced by negative behaviors. Pitfalls are creeping into their lives like a poisonous snake. Even though some youths who have fallen into a pit were fortunate to get out, others live with the consequences of their pitfall for a long time, and unfortunately, some lose their lives. At times, it seems like a healthy decision is hard to make and maintain. "Why bother to try? Whatever will be will be." Do you believe that? Will you settle for less than the best?

No way! God forbid! I have come to tell you differently. You were destined to be. God's creation is never a mistake. He has created you for a purpose, and He has placed in you the abilities to fulfill your purpose. In doing so, you can attain good success. Sometimes, you just need encouragement, guidance, and support. Be encouraged, stay positive, remain hopeful, and keep company with those who will support you in your pursuit for good success. Let self-determination become your best friend.

In this book, the voice of your company of good success speaks. You will be empowered to rise above negativity. You will be challenged to do the right thing. You will be mentored to achieve greatness. You will be given the tools to dodge the snares and traps that can harm or destroy your destiny.

My prayer is that this life guide book impacts you in such a powerful and positive way, because your life matters!

B. Courage to Go Against the Odds

In today's mode of mass communication, we hear a lot about things "going viral." Things go viral when, for instance, you take a picture of an event at your home and post it on social media to all of your contacts, your contacts then post it to their contacts, significantly increasing the number of "likes" and viewers increase. "Viral" comes from the word virus, and a "virus" is an organism that causes disease.

Yep, viral—it is not surprising that they adopted this name for the spread of information across the globe. By nature, viruses spread rapidly. While social media can be fun and entertaining, the downside is that some of the shared information is not helpful. Just like a virus that causes physical illness, viral media can cause emotional and personal pain. Posting false information about another person and sending it to hundreds of contacts can defame a person's character.

Do you find yourself enjoying gossip? Do you get those urges to know what the latest rumor around town is? Let's be honest, social media drama can be exciting, and many folks enjoy the spread of negativity and lies versus the truth. But, we all know that it would only benefit society if those desires and practices are aborted. Where are the "change agents"? It's time for some radical youths to rise up with the courage to go against the odds.

To make an impact on your generation and the generations to come, youths must rise and think differently. Why should you succumb to those issues that can be avoided? Why do you have to participate in sending harmful messages via social media? Why should you have to suffer from making poor decisions? Why do you have to repeat the mistakes of others? Why do you have to fall into a pit to learn a lesson?

In Joshua 1: 5 – 7, God encourages Joshua, as the next leader after Moses's death, to be strong and very courageous. I envision you as part of the modern-day Joshua generation movement— equipped with boldness, armed with discipline, and drenched with conviction to cross over the many obstacles of life into your promised destiny. Social media is a great communication tool, and it is one of the most used modes of influence. Use it to turn those bad viruses into good ones. Spread the good, and empower your peers to overcome pitfalls.

It is crucial for me to touch on the importance of rising up as the modern-day Joshua generation. Once you grasp the concept of escaping the pitfalls of life, you will be the greatest influence in your schools, communities, and the world. My God! How awesome that will be!

CHAPTER THREE

THE RISING GENERATION:
WHAT ARE YOU MADE UP OF?

If someone asked, "What are you made up of?" what would your response be?

When I was younger, my response would have been, "What do you mean? You are looking at me! Can't you see?"

As you know, the products we use are made from different materials. A car is built with materials such as steel, aluminum, rubber, and glass. Lumber, concrete, and bricks are used to build a house. Also, there are clothes with different types of materials and foods with multiple ingredients.

Even the masterpiece of the human body is made up of components such as blood vessels, muscles, bones, and organs. But is that all? Is there more to us? Well, I am here to let you know that the answer is yes!

As the rising generation, you have to know exactly who you are and what you are made up of. You need to know all that you are so that you will be a part of the generation that rises confidently as a whole person.

Let's see what God's Word states about your makeup.

> 1 Thessalonians 5:23 "I pray God your whole spirit and soul and body be preserved blameless unto the coming of our Lord Jesus Christ."

This verse identifies you as one person with three parts—spirit, soul, and body. Isn't that incredible?

I hear you say, "Break it down! Break it down!" Okay, here we go!

A. Youthful Spirit

Your youthful spirit comes from your heavenly creator.

> Genesis 2:7 *"Then the Lord God formed a man from the dust of the ground and breathed into his nostrils the breath of life, and the man became a living being."*

In the beginning, God formed Adam, the first man, out of the dust of the earth. He then breathed life into him. The gift of God's breath, which is His Spirit, brought life into Adam's lifeless body. To me, that was an epic moment.

It may be difficult to understand the whole event of the creation of man. The reason is that God is supernatural, and He does things that are above our way of thinking. Nevertheless, the Spirit of God was with man from the time man was created. When God breathed into Adam, the spirit of man was then created. So there you go: one part of a living human being is his/her spirit.

The spirit is the part of a person that connects and communicates with God. Praying is one way to connect with God, and reading the Holy Bible is how we learn about Him. The spirit of a person can also be disconnected from God. As we continue on the subject of spirit, soul and body, you will begin to have more insight into what you are made up of and how the parts work together for good or bad.

B. Powerful Soul

The soul is the mind, the will, and the emotions.

The soul/mind is the part of the person that thinks. "What am I going to do today? What am I going to wear?"

The soul/will is the part of a person that decides what to do. "I am going to the movies. I will wear my distressed blue jeans."

The soul/emotion is the part of the person that feels. "At the movies, I was happy because the movie was funny." The soul thinks, decides, and then the body acts.

> Matthew 22:37 "Love the Lord your God with all your heart and with all your soul and with all your mind."

This verse encourages you to love God with all your heart and soul. If your heart and soul love God, then your intention will be to do the things that please your heavenly Father. If you mess up, don't be discouraged; just work on improving your weak areas. Never give up on making things better in your life.

The soul is truly a powerful part of who we are, and it plays a very important role in preventing the pitfalls of life.

C. Awesome Body

This is the part of us that is physical. We have body parts that can be seen and internal organs that work together to keep us functioning. The five senses—seeing, smelling, feeling, hearing, and tasting—are essential for communicating to the brain.

> Genesis 5:2 "He created them male and female and blessed them. And he named them 'Mankind' when they were created."

D. The Whole You

You are a youthful spirit and a powerful soul; your body is a masterpiece of God's creation. These three parts work together to make a whole you.

Myles Monroe,[2] an evangelist and ordained minister, put it together nicely in his "Wisdom for Dominion" message, in which he spoke about how the spirit, soul, and body operate. The entire message was incredible, but I will highlight one powerful statement that he made:

"The soul can only do what it accepts from the spirit."

Earlier, I mentioned how God, who is a spirit, breathed life into man; therefore, when God speaks to us through His Word, He is actually speaking to the part of us that is our spirit.

By the way, it is important to note that our spirit can accept good from God or evil from the devil.

When the Spirit of God speaks to us, He speaks words of life and hope, but when the the devil speaks, his words are of death and destruction.

Therefore, if the soul can only do what it accepts from the spirit, it is crucial that we know which spirit we receive and accept our life instructions from.

Teens, there is so much out there to distract you and steer you away from your path to do well. You have to remain sober and alert. The devil uses every opportunity to bring a person down, lead them into a pitfall, and destroy them when they are not paying attention.

Our actions are influenced by the Spirit of God or by the devil. Which spirit is influencing you today? Which spirit is your soul paying attention to? Who are you allowing to speak into your ears? Whose instructions and advice are you embracing? What is your best friend telling you to do? Where is his/her influence coming from? These are hard questions, but they are extremely important and must be answered by you.

Now, for your spirit to listen to the right spirit, you have to know what the Word of God states. Just like your daily meals nourish your physical body so that you don't get weak and sick, God's Word acts the same. His Word is your daily spiritual food. It gives you healthy nourishment for your spiritual life.

The Word of God will help you to learn, grow, and develop a great lifestyle. Lack of prayer and not knowing the Word of God will lead to a weak spiritual life and poor decision-making.

E. Connecting the Parts

Youthful Spirit	Powerful Soul	Awesome Body
Jay read in the Bible, "Thou shall not steal."	Jay saw a nice bracelet on the teacher's desk, and she decided to listen to the Spirit of God through His Word that states, "Thou shall not steal."	Jay walked away from the desk and did not pick up the bracelet.

Previously, I mentioned that knowledge is power. Well, you have just received a high voltage of power that you are encouraged to use to infuse your life. Have you ever wondered why people do what they do, or how decisions are influenced? Now you know! It's a spirit, soul, and body thing. Therefore, bringing the whole you to function according to God's best plan for your life is my hope.

Stay on course—our journey continues, and it gets better. In the end, the whole you will be empowered to soar above the negative circumstances in life.

No - Pit - 4 - Us

ACTIVITY 2

1. Divide the number of teens reading this book into two groups.

2. Assign one of the scenarios below to each group.

3. Using the information about the spirit, soul, and body, discuss the following three questions:

    A. What are the various decisions that can be made in each scenario?

    B. Which spirit influences each decision?

    C. What is the best decision and why?

Scenario 1
While attending a high school prom, Plato walked into the restroom and found a wallet with $500 cash, credit cards, and the owner's driver's license.

Using his cell phone, Plato called two of his friends to tell them to come and see what he found. In the restroom, they discussed what to do with each of the items: the cash, the credit cards, and the ID.

Scenario 2
Serene's mom told her to go directly home after school. However, her classmates insist that she go to the library with them to study for the math test.

CHAPTER FOUR

GETTING TOGETHER:
UNDERSTANDING THE CONNECTIONS

Socializing is one of the most fun things to do. Hanging out at someone's home or playing ball on the court with your friends is what makes life fulfilling and memorable. Think about the times you've met up with friends to plan a trip, have a sleepover, head to the mall, play a sport, practice your crafts and hobbies, or watch a movie. How did you feel during those moments? What made those interactions with your friends special? What activities did you guys bond over and participate in while hanging out? One very popular activity comes to my mind when I think about hanging out with my friends. It's usually the highlight of my day. Can you guess what it is? Yep! Eating!

Whatever the occasion may be or wherever the event may be held, you can always be sure that the enjoyment of food and drinks will be involved. Oh! I'm getting hungry thinking about juicy hamburgers, crispy fries, fried chicken, pizza, donuts, and a nice cold drink.

Having said that, when socializing, there are times when a person, or a group of people will decide to participate in activities that may not be positive, safe, or beneficial. Now, we have finally arrived at the chapter of the book that focuses on two words that are very familiar to your age group: "peer pressure."

A. Peer Pressure & the Teen Brain

Peer pressure is a feeling that one must do the same things as other people of one's age and social group to be liked or respected by them.[3]

If you were pressured to do the right thing, then there would be no cause for concern, but unfortunately, peer pressures today are not all healthy. A lot of the influences are more negative than positive.

Teens, you are vulnerable to peer pressure because you are in a developmental transition. This means that you are smack in the middle between a child and an adult, and for some of you, the process of maturing and making healthy decisions is difficult. You need the tools to overcome negative peer pressure, and it's for this reason that *The Rising Generation: No - Pit - 4 - Us* has been written.

Medical experts state that the part of the brain that makes rational decisions is fully developed around the age of 25.[4] Yep! 25! That explains why teens tend to make hasty and poor decisions, especially when pressured by their peers. It is important to note that those teens who pressure you to do wrong also do not have fully developed brains; therefore, they too are making irrational decisions.

So, how do we address this complex issue? Let's go back to the profound statement: **"Knowledge is power."** Now that you know more about the developmental stage of the teenage brain as it relates to making important decisions, my advice to you is to call your company of good success for support and assistance. If you feel like you are being pressured or bullied, never be afraid to speak up. It is unhealthy to keep your thoughts, feelings, and emotions bottled up. If you feel afraid, worthless, unnoticed, or teased, or if you simply do not feel good about yourself, please do not hesitate to reach out to a positive and caring role model in your life with whom you can safely express your feelings and concerns.

I strongly encourage you to always consult a loved one with wisdom, Godly guidance, and experience, who will steer you in the right direction. Never let anyone pressure you into making a quick decision. Remember, pitfalls happen when hasty emotional decisions are made. The actions can be forgiven but not reversed.

But in the event that you ever feel pressured, have no one around to talk to, and feel trapped in a situation, always remember these few secrets that I discovered during my moments of peer pressure. These secrets always gave me the courage and strength to say no to peer pressure without any care for what people would say or think about me. Are you ready? Here it is! "I am strong, I can overcome this, and I have to protect the most important person, ME!" So, you are resilient, you are competent, and you must protect the most important person, YOU!

Finally, you can do all things through Christ who strengthens you. "All things" includes OVERCOMING negative pressures. YOU GOT THIS!

B. A Friend, An Acquaintance, A Stranger

Let's talk a little about a word that people most often misinterpret: friend. It is important to note that there are three types of people you may encounter in your life: 1) a friend, 2) an acquaintance, and 3) a stranger.

Many people use the word "friend" very loosely, as my friend Greta would say. I find it very necessary to define each category, and I hope that at the end, you will have a better understanding of the people within your surroundings and the part that each of them plays in your life.

Friend: Friendship is such an important relationship, so I will expand on its qualities some more. A friend is someone who knows you, and you know them. Both of you know each other's likes and dislikes. You are aware of each other's strengths and weaknesses. You know each other's goals and aspirations. A friend is good to you. A friend corrects you when you need to be corrected. A friend supports you and will not harm you. A friend will not lead you in the wrong path. A friend helps you to succeed in life.

Acquaintance: An acquaintance is someone you know but who is not close to you. You may know their name and where they live, but that's it. That person may be a classmate or your neighbor five blocks away.

Stranger: A stranger is a person you don't know and have never personally met.

The take-home message is, a friend will never pressure you into doing things that will be harmful to your present and destructive to your future.

CHAPTER FIVE

THE FACE OF PEER PRESSURE

A. Booze, Snooze, Lose

The face of negative peer pressure is sometimes attractive. When someone is being pressured into doing something that is harmful, the ugliness of the outcome is masked. That is why it is very important for you to be aware of, recognize, and avoid potential pitfalls.

After the dress rehearsal for the play, Pep said, "I'm hungry; let's get something to eat," so the group decided to order pizza and soda. Slim offered to pick up the food. On the way back, Slim made a detour to ask one of his friends to purchase a couple bottles of liquor for him. Slim was only 15 years old and looked 15, so he would not have been able to purchase the alcoholic beverages on his own. Shortly after, Slim pranced back into the studio. He was delightedly carrying three large boxes of scrumptious pizza, three liters of Pepsi soda, and one brown bag with two tall bottles in it. Pep had not eaten for the entire day; therefore, she grabbed the pepperoni pizza and dug in.

Before Pep ate her first slice, she asked, "What's in the brown bag?"

Slim: "Something to make you happy."

Pep: "Oh, really?"

Slim: "Yep! Let me help you. I will pour some for everyone."

Pep: "Soda is good enough for me."

Slim: "We worked so hard practicing for the play. Come on. Enjoy yourself."

(Pep hits Slim on his shoulder and says)

Pep: "You are trying to get us drunk!"

Slim: "And so what? A little drink will not hurt. Grow up and take a sip."

Is this real or not? Oh yes, this scenario is as real as it gets. Daily, teenagers are challenged by their peers to drink. Whether it's beer, brandy, whiskey, vodka, wine, or rum, it's all alcohol. When teens are offered alcohol, the risk they face is usually not mentioned.

Negative peer pressure has a way of boosting one's curiosity and increasing their temptation. This nuisance, *peer pressure*, usually shows up at social events or when someone is emotionally vulnerable, weak, sad, hurt, lonely, helpless, or wanting to fit in.

Here Are Some Facts

Alcohol is a drug that is commonly abused, and it adversely affects the body. Using alcohol for a long period of time can affect the heart, stomach, liver, pancreas, kidney, bones, and even hearing. But, for our purpose, we will focus on the immediate effect of alcohol on the brain.

WEBMD[5] gives one of the best explanation of the effects of alcohol on the brain:

"Thirty seconds after your first sip, alcohol races into your brain. It slows down the chemicals and pathways that your brain cells use to send messages. That alters your mood, slows your reflexes, and throws off your balance. You also can't think straight, which you may not recall later, because you'll struggle to store things in long-term memory."

Not being able to think straight, losing control of what you do, not knowing where you are, and putting your safety and life in jeopardy are serious consequences of consuming alcohol as a teen. I am confident that as you become more aware and educated on the negative consequences of alcohol, you will be empowered to make the right decisions when you are offered booze.

Continuing with the issues regarding the negative impacts of alcohol use in teens, the Center For Disease Control and Prevention[6] states,

"In 2013, there were approximately 119,000 emergency rooms visits by persons aged 12 to 21 for injuries and other conditions linked to alcohol."

As a former emergency medical technician and then an emergency room nurse, I have personally observed that many of the emergency room visits were due to alcohol overdose.

Taking a chance on a drink is taking a chance on your life and future. One may never plan to get into trouble, but once teens get together to try something tempting or risky, things usually spiral out of control. Remember that logical thinking and brain development we mentioned earlier? Keep that at the forefront of your mind when making decisions, and challenge your peers to do the same.

Saying no, walking away, turning the glass down, not taking an open drink from someone, whatever it may take, just do it, because you may be saving yourself from the negative consequences of underage drinking.

Let's look at some of those weighty problems that come along with underage drinking. The Center For Disease Control and Prevention[7] states that youths who drink alcohol are most likely to experience:

- School problems, such as higher absence and poor or failing grades

- Social problems, such as fighting and lack of participation in youth activities

- Legal problems, such as arrest for driving or physically hurting someone while drunk

- Physical problems, such as hangovers or illnesses

- Unwanted, unplanned, and unprotected sexual activity

- Disruption of normal growth and sexual development

- Physical and sexual assault

- Higher risk for suicide and homicide

- Alcohol-related car crashes and other unintentional injuries, such as burns, falls, and drowning

- Memory problems

- Abuse of other drugs

- Changes in brain development that may have lifelong effects

- Death from alcohol poisoning

Because of the risk, you have to be prepared to make firm decisions. You must be aware of the danger. You have to know when to say "no" and walk away.

> Proverbs 20:1 *"Wine is a mocker and beer a brawler; whoever is led astray by them is not wise."*

Consuming alcohol can cause you to lose some of the most valued things in life. I challenge you to escape this pitfall and encourage your peers to do the same. You are destined to be great, successful, and all that you can be.

B. Haste, Taste, Waste

I was faced with a situation in an uncomfortable place,
involved in the act, feeling trapped,
it was not an afternoon nap.
Friends painted the picture so I can foretaste,
that as I soon realized, it's better to wait.

In my feeling of disgrace,
I wish that time could erase, but God had it so,
that His Grace filled my space.

Healed and restored with no time to waste,
I choose to move on with a new slate.
Embracing the right, listening to good advice,
seeking the best,
and walking away from the rest.

Sex is a beautiful, intimate experience created by God, but the world has altered God's plan for sex and twisted it into an ugly mess.

Many television shows, commercials, movies, music, books, and dances are preoccupied with corrupted sexual content, and they are negatively influencing the behaviors of teens.

The aforementioned poem depicts how a teen was pressured into sex that she was not ready for. After the fact, she acknowledged that she could have waited. The way that teens rush into sex, you would think it's on clearance. Whether it's in a bed, a truck, the backseat of a car, under a bridge, behind the school building, at a party, or in a smelly restroom, they find a way.

But hold up. You don't need to frustrate your little heads any longer. There is no close-out sale! There is no clearance rack! Sex has always been, and it will always be. It is not going anywhere. Relax! You have more than enough time to get your portion of sex in the right way, at the right time, and under the right conditions—no sneaking, no hiding, no dodging, no dipping, no peeping, no sinning. There will come a time when you can have sex freely without feeling guilty or regretful in the end. I do hope that this makes you feel much better.

Let's hear what God, your creator, says about this act.

> 1 Thessalonians 4:3 "For this is the will of God, even your sanctification, that ye should abstain from fornication."

Fornication is having sex outside of marriage. God wants His best for you, so He urges you not to fornicate, and in doing so, you are sanctified. Sanctification simply means to be clean.

You may ask, "Why is it important to be clean?" Well, that is God's best plan for your life, and it is His standard to enter his eternal Kingdom.

Finally, what I find to be very important is that your mind and memory are protected when you refrain from engaging in sex at a young age. Crowding your memory with past negative experiences should be avoided. The more involved someone gets in activities that are unhealthy and not right for them, the more they will think about it, and they will have to deal with the memory and hurt throughout their life. As a result, spiritual and psychological counseling may be needed to help the person overcome the pain. Avoid bad and unhealthy behaviors to prevent collections of unhealthy memories!

Call to Abstinence

How can you prepare yourself to abstain from sex at such a young age? Here are some suggestions that I believe will assist you:

First: Know

Know what God says about sex. We just touched on that subject, so you have started on the right track.

Second: Accept

Accept God's plan for your life. The devil has his plan, and his plan is to get you to disobey God. The devil's plan is to get you to misuse your body. God's plan is to set you free from enslaving your body and mind into something that you are not ready for. Don't let anyone tell you that you have to engage in sex as a teenager, because you don't. YOU HAVE A CHOICE! YOU CAN SAY NO! Accept the best plan, because you deserve the best.

Third: Commit

Commit to practicing what you know and what you have accepted. Since 1 Thessalonians 4:3 states to abstain from fornication, then you should commit to doing that. Make a promise to yourself and work towards it. This does not mean that you will be perfect, but the whole idea is to consciously make a decision to try your best.

Fourth: Disconnect

Birds of a feather flock together, so disconnect yourself from people whose primary goal is to get you to break your commitment to abstain. Remember that some movies, music, dances, places, and social media contain things that will provoke and open up your appetite for sex. Removing yourself from these environments and hanging out in neutral settings that promote healthy conduct is the path to take. Just in case you were wondering what you will miss, give me a few moments, and I will let you know exactly what you are missing out on when you don't have sex as a teen.

But, before we get there, let me talk to some of you who have had sex or who are having sex. It is not the end of the world. God loves you, and He will forgive and restore you. The Bible states that all of us have sinned and come short of the glory of God, but if and when we sin, God forgives us. Once you ask Him to forgive you, He certainly will.

NEVER lose hope and NEVER beat up on yourself because you have already had sex. The most important thing is that when you ask

God to forgive you, he forgives you and it's done. Moving forward, you have to remember to disconnect. Don't go backward. God has your back. He will strengthen you. You have to mean what you say and work towards accomplishing that goal.

Teens, as a professional nurse, I am fully aware that some of you are having sex. On a daily basis, I counsel and take care of clients who have contracted a sexually transmitted disease, and these clients are usually very angry and regretful. Therefore, it is important for me to interject that having a safe sexual relationship is important. At your age, having sex creates too many issues that are quite burdensome for you to deal with; therefore, talk to someone in your circle of good success, whether your parent, school counselor, nurse, or provider at the clinic. Their job is to provide the best information to help you make the best decision for your life. They will provide you with education on safe sex and family planning.

Skipping Sex! We're Missing Out on What?
Here is a list of some of the issues teens can face when engaging in sexual activities at a young age. Some of these issues are so complex that if I took the time to elaborate on each one, it would take a whole chapter for each point. A moment of pleasure can end up leading to a lifetime of hardship.

Pregnancy	Lack of support	Lying
Abortion	Guilt	Sleep disorder
Addiction	Shame	Psychological disturbance
Perversion – oral and anal sex	Regret	Financial issues
Problems with family relationships	Worry	Sexually transmitted diseases
Reproductive problems	Long-term health issues	Problems with schoolwork

Gosh! Any takers? I thought you would say no. This is the reality, teens. While some teens may not go through most of the issues listed, the risk of experiencing any of them is great.

Adults who have your best interest at heart, and adults who have gone through the trials of engaging in sex as a teen, only want to spare you from this pitfall, but it's up to you to do your best to spare yourself. I would suggest that you do everything in your power to avoid this, because when you do, your life will be less complicated. Always remember, the fewer complications you have, the more you can focus on building a better future.

On the other hand, some of you reading this book may be experiencing the issues listed here. I want you to know that hope, healing, restoration, and recovery are available to you. It is up to you to take hold of them. I always say, "Where there is life, there is hope." There is hope to turn around and move in a different direction. Do not expect things to get better for you if you have not changed the way you do things. If you continue to have sex as a teen, then the consequences may multiply and make your life even more difficult.

One beautiful thing about God is that when we fall away from Him, He is willing to take us in His loving arms and get us back on track. Yes, indeed, you can get back on track. Call your company of good success and allow them to assist and guide you on the road to a new start.

Here are some of the things that I suggest you do:

1. Be hopeful that things will get better. Never, ever tell yourself that you are a failure.

2. Commit to following God and His plan for your life.

3. Surround yourself with people who are doing the right things and who are willing to support your decision to abstain from sex.

4. Have an open conversation with your family. Ask your family for their support.

5. Empower yourself to abstain from sex by:

   • Attending a sexual abstinence program in your community.

   • Making a promise to yourself not to have sex again until the right time, with the right person, under right circumstances. Put this promise as a reminder in your room, schoolbook, cell phone, wherever you choose.

   • Listening to clean music.

   • Looking at clean movies.

   • Reading clean books.

   • Monitoring what you view on social media carefully.

   • Staying away from secluded places.

If you don't remember anything else, remember this: you don't have to see everything, hear everything, go everywhere, taste everything, or touch everything. Engaging in everything and not being selective in what you see, hear, taste or touch could be detrimental. It is important that you ask God to guide you in all that you do. Don't be driven by alcohol and sex. Take the wheel and steer your life in the right direction. You got this! Yes, you can! Your life is valuable and precious to God.

As it relates to abstaining from sex, trust me, you are not going to die. I have never heard of anyone's death certificate stating their cause of death was due to a lack of sex. You will be all right without teen sex! That's a promise!

Much has been said, and I hope that you are now challenged and empowered to rise above the pitfalls of drinking alcohol and engaging in sexual activities at this young age. I remain optimistic that you will also encourage your friends to join you in your pursuit of self-management, because it is WORTH IT ALL!

It is my prayer that instead of boozing, snoozing, and losing or making haste to taste and waste your most precious and valuable asset—your body—use it to honor and glorify God. Skipping sex and refusing to drink alcohol as a teen is a decision you will never, ever regret!

No - Pit - 4 - Us
ACTIVITY 3

For this activity, create four groups.

Group 1
Have the most talented poet read, "Haste, Taste, Waste," and have someone else elaborate on the meaning of the poem.

Group 2
Discuss some of the valuable things in life you can lose if you indulge in drinking alcohol and getting drunk.

Group 3
Read the scenario and respond.

A friend takes you out on a date to the movies. When you get there, you realize that the movie is a story about two lovers, and it's three hours long and rated "R" for sexual content. After the movie, the plan is for both of you to go for a ride along the countryside road.

Complete the following:

1. Write down the recipe for the pitfalls into fornication, and share it with the group.

2. What are some of the strategies you can use to prevent falling into the pitfall of sex before marriage?

Group 4
List, research, and discuss some of the other peer pressures a teen can experience, including the use of opioid drugs, crystal meth, sexting, e-cigarettes, risky challenges, etc. List some consequences for each.

CHAPTER SIX

C-FACTOR CHECKLIST

C-Factor Checklist—quite an unusual phrase. Well, in 2010, my oldest daughter gave the salutatorian speech to her high school graduating class, and her speech was all about the C-Factor Checklist. Many people have creative ideas and would love to share them with others. The C-Factor Checklist was an original, and she presented her message to a resilient and dynamic class. About 300 students attentively listened as she delivered a timely, relevant, and profound address. She provided her classmates with the essential wisdom as they were getting ready to leave their parents' nest to plunge into the big world of opportunities and experiences—good and bad. The "C-Factor Checklist" speaks about three "C's": Company, Confidence, and Choice.

My daughter designed the C-Factor Checklist as a guide to help her and her graduating classmates through the challenges of life. As they separated from the physical supervision of their parents to settle into college life, the military, trade schools, the work force, or even relationships, she summarized what most parents would reiterate to their children before leaving home.

A. Good Company

The first "C" represents good company. This means choosing friends and those you associate with wisely. She stated that you learn how to choose good company from the instructions, wisdom, and experiences of those who love you the most. Those people are your company of good success: company of family, company of friends, and extended company. As I indicated before, your company of good success can provide great instructions on how to avoid bad relationships and embrace good company. Most importantly, the decision to choose good company comes from the Word of God, where it states in Proverbs 13:20, "He that walketh with wise men shall be wise: but a companion of fools shall be destroyed."

I know, the word "fool" can seem a bit harsh, but being that the Word was written in a different era with a different culture, the underlying message is this: when choosing your companions, pay attention to the path that they walk. Are they continuously making poor choices despite the known consequences? Are they always in trouble, disrespectful, and seeming to have no regard for the success of their own life? Or are they driven, ambitious, and focused? Are they positive, loving, and giving? Today, a fool would be someone who fits the definition of insanity—doing the same thing over and over but expecting a different outcome. They make repeated mistakes and may not have the desire to do better. For them, doing the right thing is not important.

The Bible states not to keep company with them because you will be destroyed. No, not literally destroyed—I hope not—but destroyed in the sense that whatever poor decisions the people you hang around with continuously make may steer you off the path that God has created for you to attain your best life. Do not feel guilty when separating yourself from bad company. Remember, the most important person you have a duty to protect is YOU. Do what is necessary to preserve your success, but also remember to continuously pray for them.

You know that saying "always look for the silver lining"? Separating from bad company may be painful, because these are people that you love and may consider your friends at the moment. However, the bright side to this process of growth is this: you get the opportunity to be a good example for them. You get to show them the optimal side of life. The life where they can be whole, obedient, respectful, studious, focused, and productive, and still have tons of fun with good company. You never know, one day your life may cause them to change theirs. As a rule, good company keeps you out of trouble.

Note these three points:

1. Company that engages in unlawful acts or behavior is not good company. Good company does not practice wrong doings.

2. Company that disobeys their parents is not good company. Good company honors their parents.

3. Company that is not progressive and does not show ambition to grow is not good company. Good company is all about getting better and striving for good success.

You are strongly encouraged to keep company with wise teenagers. Yes, they may be hard to find, but they are out there. That wise teenager is closer than you think—you are one of them! It is not by accident that you are reading this book. By the mere fact that you are reading this book, you have already been inducted into that pool of good company. Share the information you learned in this life-changing guide and let the good company grow across your neighborhoods and schools.

"Keep company with those who make you better." -English saying

B. Strong Confidence

My daughter's speech went on to the second "C," which represents strong confidence. She explained to her classmates that it was necessary for all of them to develop inner strength so that they could be self-motivated to accomplish their goals. As I reminisce on the speech, the construction of a house comes to mind; I will stick to the basics and leave the intricate details of building the house to you aspiring architects, contractors, and engineers.

The architect draws the plan, and the contractor uses the plan as a road map to build the house. At the beginning phase of building the house, many things are done concurrently, but one of the most significant parts is the foundation. The foundation is the floor, and that holds all the weight, so the floor has to be strong.

If the floor is constructed poorly, as time goes by and more weight is added, the floor will get weaker and weaker. It will begin to sink, crack, slant, or even cave in.

Let's look at the word "confidence."

The Cambridge Dictionary defines confidence as "having little doubt about yourself and your abilities, or a feeling of trust in someone or something."[8]

You see that? Confidence is trust in your ability. God created you with plenty of talent, abilities, and strength. Having strong confidence is trusting yourself and the ability that God has placed in you to do whatever needs to be done.

Strong confidence comes from the foundation of the Word of God. The Bible states in Philippians 4:13, "I can do all things through Christ who strengthens me."

> Ephesians 2:10 "For we are God's handiwork, created in Christ Jesus to do good works, which God prepared in advance for us to do."

God has prepared you to do good work.

This is a self-empowerment moment; tell yourself, "Yes, I can." Yes, you can have strong confidence.

The hit song in the Christian arena during the time I am writing this life guide is "I Know Who I Am" by Sinach. What a powerful song! The lyrics are self-motivating and they declare what God says about you.

Do you know that words create? In the beginning, God said, "Let there be light," and there was light. God spoke things into being, and so today, He has given us that authority on the earth to speak, and it happens.

Proverbs 18:21, "Death and life are in the power of the tongue."

When you sing, "I Know Who I Am," it puts you in a position to conquer. Why? Because the spoken WORD brings results.

Build your confidence in what God says about you. Just as negative and derogatory words can destroy people, positive and empowering words can build people in the same way. You have the ability and responsibility to strengthen your emotions, thinking, and attitude based on God's Word. The ball is in your court. Here are some more scriptures to help you:

- Psalm 139:14, "I will praise thee; for I am fearfully and wonderfully made: marvelous are thy works; and that my soul knoweth right well."

- Deuteronomy 28:13, "And the LORD shall make thee the head, and not the tail; and thou shalt be above only, and thou shalt not be beneath."

- Romans 8:37, "Nay, in all these things we are more than conquerors through him that loved us."

A homeowner has strong confidence in his house if it is built on a strong foundation. So too can you have strong confidence in your life if your life is built on a strong foundation. The same way a house can collapse if the foundation is not strong, you can collapse if your foundation is not strong. So tightly embrace all the positive things that God says about you, and you will be a "force of confidence" to be reckoned with.

C. Best Choice

The third "C" represents best choice. What is the best choice when faced with a difficult decision? What should be done when you find yourself stuck between a rock and a hard place? I believe a combination of education, wise counsel, critical-thinking skills, and life experiences are great resources on which to base the best choice.

Let's look at this situation:

Pinky, a high school junior, has to decide which summer program to attend. She wants to study business and work in the field of marketing. She has one more summer to better prepare herself for college. Salmon and fries are her favorite foods, and she loves surfing the Internet while sitting on the beach. Which one of the three summer programs would you choose for her to attend?

Program #1
Located in Alaska, where salmon is in abundance, all expenses are paid, and the summer courses are in the fields of fishing and agriculture.

Program #2
Located in the Caribbean, where the beaches are so beautiful, all expenses are paid, and the summer courses are in the field of political science.

Program #3
Located in her home town, costs $3,000, and the summer courses are in the field of marketing.

It is decision-making time! Which summer program is the best choice?

Before moving on, think about the entire scenario and choose a program. Once you have selected the summer camp for Pinky to attend, continue reading.

Okay, are you ready? Here we go! To make the best choice, we have to formulate some questions and answer them.

Questions:

1. What is Pinky's goal?

2. Why is she attending the summer program?

3. How many opportunities does she have to attend a summer program before attending college?

Answers:

1. To attend a summer program.

2. To better prepare herself to study marketing in college.

3. One more summer.

Decision-making time:

Pinky's main goal is to attend a summer program that offers a course that will prepare her for studies in marketing. Attending the summer program at home is the best choice based on the most important thing she wants to accomplish. Traveling to either Alaska or the Caribbean sounds exciting and would definitely be a great trip, but going to either of those two places will not help her to accomplish her immediate goal.

When faced with a tough situation where you have to make a choice, here are some tips that may help:

1. Never make a hasty or quick decision. Always give yourself time to think.

2. When making a decision, you have to weigh the advantages and disadvantages of each side. What can happen if I do this, or what can happen if I do the other? What is the good in it for me?

3. When making a decision, set your priority. What is the most important thing to do first?

4. Ask someone for advice. You can learn from other people's experiences, knowledge, and expertise. Proverbs 11:14 states, "Where no counsel is, the people fall, but in the multitude of counselors, there is safety."

I mentioned the C-Factor Checklist because I believe when all three—good company, strong confidence, and best choice—become a part of how you run your camp, that is when negative peer pressure has no control over you. Your strong confidence stands tall, the best decisions begin to roll out, and your circle of good company is established. Challenge yourself, knock your socks off, and surprise yourself. May the principles of the C-Factor Checklist be established in your life.

CHAPTER SEVEN

GUARDING YOUR FUTURE

A. Sensing the Pit and Preventing the Fall

Have you ever been in a situation where you were asked to do something, and the whole idea did not feel right? Did you ask yourself some questions about it?

Well, I really hope that you did. However, if you did not, keep reading, and I will provide you with information that will help you to figure it out. The uncomfortable feeling you feel in a particular situation is that nagging sensation that we all call our "gut feeling." It is letting you know that something is not right. Something is not adding up. A piece of the puzzle is missing. This does not make sense.

Some cultures use other idioms like "my intuition told me," "my spirit is not settled," or even "I see a red flag." That sensing comes from the wisdom of God's Word as well as the disciplines of learning right from wrong. Regardless of the phrase, they all mean something is up, and that something is usually not good. Therefore, the takeaway message is that "sensing" or that "feeling" should never be ignored. Ignoring that sensing could lead to an undesirable outcome.

1. Consequences of Pitfalls

The core of *The Rising Generation: No - Pit - 4 - Us* is to help you and your peers to avoid the pitfalls of life. Remember, pitfalls are hidden or unsuspected dangers or difficulties. Pitfalls are traps and snares.

Getting arrested and sentenced to time behind bars is a consequence of stealing. Stealing is the pitfall. Teenage pregnancy and contracting a sexually transmitted disease are consequences of having sex. Sex is the pitfall. Being expelled from school is the consequence of cheating on a test. Cheating is the pitfall.

When someone falls into a pit, they can become trapped, and here is what can happen:

1. A person can become addicted. They will continue to repeat the same mistake over and over again.

2. Their progress is put on hold. High school graduation could be delayed because of a dumb pitfall.

3. Life becomes very difficult. It's hard to get a job if you have a history of stealing.

4. Dreams and goals could be aborted. A young man is disqualified from enrolling in a specific program because of his former drug use. A young lady could be ineligible to compete in a pageant because she was caught shoplifting.

5. The behavioral health of a person could be negatively impacted by stress. People could become very depressed and even suicidal.

6. People can lose their lives. A drunk driver could cause an accident, resulting in his death or the death of his passengers, occupants of the other vehicles, or pedestrians.

Taking even one risk can subject your life to danger, place your career in jeopardy, threaten your future aspirations, and create a family crisis. The question is, "Is it worth taking the risk?" Is it worth taking the chance just to fit in? Is it more important for you to do it just to say you did it and to score one with your peers? Is it worth taking the chance just to please someone else? There comes a time when you have to make a selfish decision because when it's all done, you are the one that has to deal with the backlash.

At your age, your time should be spent learning, playing, and having clean fun. Take healthy risks, such as enrolling in a competition, running for office in your class, competing in a sport, or going on an ice or jet skiing excursion with your family.

Challenge your creativity, find a project to work on, invent something, organize a class trip, join an organization, or become an entrepreneur.

Sharpen your skills and talents by joining a band or sports team, draw, paint, create a club.

Enjoy your youth, have friends over and watch movies, play board games, have a cooking competition, try new foods, organize a theme park day with friends, go to the beach, go sailing, attend a concert, enroll in a summer camp, attend youth rallies, hang out at the mall, or go on fishing trips.

Of course, Dad and Mom have to be in on most of these plans, and once they know that you are working towards healthy relationships and activities, they will be happy to support you.

The point is that there are many healthy activities for you to do, and they won't spoil your reputation and create consequences of pitfalls. Staying out of messy and risky behaviors and building a successful life for you and your future family are what *The Rising Generation: No - Pit - 4 - Us* is rooting for.

Having said all of that, let's look at some ways to recognize potential pitfalls.

Please note that there may be more ways to identify the possibility of pitfalls, but these are the nine questions that I believe, if asked, will help you to make some of the best decisions to prevent them.

2. How to Identify Potential Pitfalls

1. Is it a secret? I am not talking about a surprise birthday party. I am talking about something you cannot tell anyone before,

during, or after the event. This is a highly suspicious situation. To avoid a pitfall, getting involved in such secrets is to be avoided. Get help immediately; reach out to your company of good success.

2. Do you have enough knowledge and details about the activity? Having full knowledge of what you are getting into, where you are going, who will be there, why it is happening, and when and how it will happen is important. Since you are a minor, your parents and family need to know about your whereabouts and what you are engaging in. If you don't know and you can't tell them, that is a red flag. Being aware of and avoiding these types of situations is important to your safety and overall wellbeing.

3. Will you be isolated? Will you be taken to a place where you can't make calls or contact anyone? Your safety net—company of good success—is distant. Do not rush into a situation where you may be secluded. Stop! Think! Ask questions. If you will be hauled away to some hidden place, get help.

4. Is this a risky operation? Will your life be in danger? Scrutinize the whole situation—don't jump into anything. Always remember to step back, take a deep breath, and think. You can do it. Your final decision and what you do will play a great part in the outcome.

5. Do you feel forced? Is it a situation where you are compelled to make a decision quickly? Is it a big rush? Be very careful with these types of situations. This type of trap creates a lot of pressure and anxiety. The perpetrator will probably make you feel like you will miss out if you don't do whatever it is now. Don't fall for it. Never feel like you have to decide on the spot. Always give yourself time to make a wise decision.

6. Do you feel restricted or controlled? Are you told what to do, what to say, where to go? Do you have a choice or a voice in the whole relationship? A controlling situation is very

uncomfortable. It's like a slave and master. You have no rights and no say. You are not free to make a decision. This situation is never healthy. Pay close attention; do not embrace, entertain, or nurture a controlling relationship.

7. Are you being bribed? When receiving something from someone, make sure there are no strings attached. Usually, when strings are attached, the person who is giving something wants something back in return. Also, someone may be asked to do something wrong, and then they will be given a reward. Don't let getting nice things come at the expense of wrong behavior or a crime. Don't let your body be used for the reward of things. You are more valuable than that. Get what you want and what you need in the right way and from the right people. A word to the wise is sufficient.

8. Is the activity illegal? I believe the conjuring up of illegal and ungodly activities is behind the "yes" to the proceeding seven questions. If someone answers yes to the previous questions, more than likely something bad will follow. Guard your life and your future plans by evading illegal activities.

9. What value or virtue is in this for me? Will I gain anything good or positive from this? Will this whole thing add quality to my life? Will it benefit me in the long run? Can I brag about it? Will this make me a better person? Is God pleased with this? If the answers to these questions are no, then run for your life. Do not get entangled with anything that will bring you down. Do not get involved in anything that will not add value to your life.

In a previous chapter, I mentioned that I am included in your company of good success. Therefore, I have outlined some of the most important steps to help you avoid pitfalls and undesirable consequences.

Never let this information go—hold on to it for dear life. With God's help, you will be able to escape the pits and plots that the devil has created to destroy you. Once you have a glimpse of a pitfall, you can then make a conscious effort to steer your life away from it. Do not walk into a pit; walk into a life of great opportunities and positive rewards.

B. The Best Secret Place

As we continue on the topic of guarding your future, I must conclude with the ultimate, most powerful and sure protection of one's future. There is no better place to be secure than in the secret place of the Most High God.

> <u>Psalm 91:1</u> *"He that dwelleth in the secret place of the most High shall abide under the shadow of the Almighty."*

Dwelling or living under God's protection is knowing God's Word, speaking and believing what God says about you, and doing what His Word says to do. Using God's Word to guide your life is the best decision you can ever make. In doing so, you will certainly put up a wall of defense around your life. Criminal activities, pornography, the use of drugs and alcohol, lying, stealing, cheating, and even prostitution will not easily influence you. God's Holy Spirit empowers you to resist the works of the flesh.

It is important to note that there are times when people make mistakes, and they have to deal with the consequences of those mistakes. We might say, "That's life." But the good thing about life is that we can also learn from our mistakes and determine in our hearts to do better. Right? Mistakes are meant for learning, not for repetition.

When you dwell in the secret place of the Most High, you are protected from the dangers of life. What does this mean? The secret place of the Most High is in His presence. How do you get into God's presence? Well, it's a daily relationship. Praying, reading God's Word, filling your heart and environment with praise and worship songs, engaging in Godly and appropriate dance, drama, movies, and social events; these create the atmosphere for God's presence to dwell.

Just imagine being in an environment where everyone is strung out on drugs, drinking alcohol, and engaging in group sex. Tell me, who or what is influencing those behaviors? Without a doubt, we all know it is not Jesus.

God's presence through His Son Jesus Christ brings righteousness, peace, and joy in the Holy Ghost. There is clean fun in His presence—no hangovers, no regrets, no worries. The presence of God is where living life begins, and life is fulfilled. The Word of God protects, preserves, and delivers. God stands guard with His holy angels to defend you.

For the youths who are experiencing issues with love, acceptance, and support, I need you to know that sex, drugs, alcohol, money, and fame all mask or cover the true pain that you are feeling. These things do not take away the deep hurt that you are going through. Engaging in these activities and lifestyles will only make your situation worse, and that does not have to happen.

There is hope, and there is a different way to live your life. You have a choice to make your future better. Turn your life, goals, ambitions, circumstances, addictions, and desires over to Jesus. He will bring you hope and healing. Changing your environment is important. Re-creating the company that you keep is your next step. Reaching out to a church for help, contacting the social services department in your area, and talking to your school counselor are all important steps that you can take to help you through your pain and process to guard your future.

Every morning when you wake up, ask God to dispatch His ministering angels of protection to keep you safe, and He will answer your sincere prayer. This is a sure way to protect your future.

Scriptures of Protection

> *Psalm 46:1 "God is our refuge and strength, a very present help in trouble."*

> *Psalm 18: 2 "The LORD is my rock, and my fortress and my deliverer; my God, my strength, in whom I will trust..."*

> *Psalm 3:3 "But you, LORD, are a shield around me, my glory, the One who lifts my head high."*

C. Things vs. Wisdom

> *Proverbs 3:13, 14 "Happy is the man that findeth wisdom, and the man that getteth understanding. For the merchandise of it is better than the merchandise of silver, and the gain thereof than fine gold."*

While valuable things are nice to have, wisdom is better than designer bags, expensive jewelry, and luxurious clothing. The above verse clearly states that if you apply wisdom in your everyday decision-making, you will be happy. Wearing all your trendy clothes to a party and not having the wisdom to be safe at that party is pointless. Don't get me wrong, I love me some fashionable outfits as well.

We all need wisdom to make the right decision, and I believe that at this point in this book, you have already begun to put some things in place concerning how you are going to handle your affairs from now on.

- Wisdom is using experiences, knowledge, and counsel to go in the best direction.

- Wisdom is learning from others' mistakes and making a decision not to make the same mistakes.

- Wisdom is God's Word.

To help guard your future, check out the wisdom of God. Learn and practice what God's Word says. Always remember, if you are not sure what to do, take a timeout to call your support systems and get their advice. They will do their best to lead you on the right course.

D. Action Today, See Results Tomorrow

If you live with grandparents or hang with older folks, you may have heard these sayings: "Whatever you do today will tell on you tomorrow," "What you sow you will reap," "If you make your bed, you will lie in it." All of these old-folk sayings mean that whatever you do today, you will have to deal with the consequences of those actions tomorrow, whether good or bad.

1. Kurt and His Pitfall

Kurt attended Great Learning High School in Smith Bay during the ninth and tenth grades. He was a great artist, and he helped the school complete many murals around the campus, but Kurt had a temper. In spite of the many counseling sessions and family meetings, he did not change the way he dealt with his classmates. He was a real bully; it had to be his way or no way at all. He got into many fights and was suspended as a result.

For eleventh and twelfth grades, Kurt transferred to a new school to finish up his high school education. As he was completing some of his college applications to study art, the school he really wanted to attend asked for a letter of character from his ninth and tenth grades counselors.

Kurt froze! *Letter of reference! Gosh! I had so many fights—who will write a good letter for me?* Yes, it's true. What you do today will come back to haunt you tomorrow. Did Kurt think about protecting his future when he was acting up? Most likely, he did not.

This is why I am sharing the information in this life guide. It is important for you to exhibit positive behavior while enjoying your youth, simply because your history remains connected to you. No one is perfect. We all can make mistakes, but being aware, alert,

47

mindful, strategic, responsible, and purposeful will help you make the best decision to protect yourself now and in the future.

E. Setting Boundaries

Many homes and businesses have guard dogs or security alarms. These security systems may be placed in front of or around the homes or businesses to prevent criminals from entering and to protect the occupants from damage and burglary. They also prevent loss of property and even life. When I googled the definition of boundary, here is what I found: "A boundary is something that indicates or fixes a limit or extent."[9]

So the guard dogs and security systems create the limits for where the criminal can go. The intention is to prevent the intruder from going past the dogs or security system. Those systems set the limit. Don't come any further. Do not cross over. Do not come into my house or business; you are not welcome.

In life, if boundaries are not set, anything and everything can walk right into your personal space and make you uncomfortable, and the intruder can hurt or violate you. To better grasp the concept of setting boundaries, let's look around our community and see what we find.

1. Beach – At the beach, a buoy is placed in the water to let people know not to swim beyond a specific point. If a swimmer goes beyond the buoy, he/she runs the risk of getting into trouble, and the lifeguard may not be able to help her/him.

2. Construction Site – Barricades are erected to alert people not to go beyond the barrier. An injury is imminent if an intruder goes past the line. A person can fall into a six-foot hole, or a stock of lumber can fall, causing a severe injury. Ouch!

3. Amusement Park – If a ride such as the "runaway-train" can aggravate a back injury, cause problems for a pregnant woman, or create a crisis for a person with a sick heart, the

theme park will post signs along the line leading to the ride. The sign will state, "Warning! If you have back problems, if you are pregnant, or if you have a heart condition, do not board this ride." Once the warning signs are ignored, and the person proceeds to hop on, then whatever happens is on them.

The buoy, barricades, and signs are all boundaries, and boundaries are used not only to warn but also to protect. So don't pass the float, don't climb over or go around the barricade, and certainly don't ignore the signs.

As a young tender plant, as my cousin Pastor Fernando Leonard would say, you can also set boundaries in your life. You have to introduce buoys, barricades, or signs to remind you that danger is beyond a certain point. You don't have to personally experience everything in life to know what the outcome will be. The risk of experiencing every single thing for yourself is not smart and can lead to a collection of baggage. The consequences of pitfalls become baggage that equates to issues, stress, mess, and nothing less. The baggage can be small, medium, or large, but it all can be quite cumbersome to carry through life.

People accumulate baggage every day because they have not set boundaries for themselves.

Earlier, we spoke about how to recognize potential pitfalls, so once you recognize them, begin to create your security systems and don't allow anyone or anything to cross those lines.

Here are a few tips for setting up boundaries to guard your life:

1. Consciously set goals. Too many people live life day after day, and whatever happens, happens. Your life and future are too important for you to live carelessly and aimlessly.

2. Write your goals down and sign the paper. There is something significant about writing. It makes things official.

3. <u>Post</u> your goals. Whether in your bedroom, bathroom, schoolbook, put it up. Posting acts as a reminder to follow through.

4. <u>Pray</u> about your goals. Ask God to help you accomplish them.

5. <u>Talk about it</u>. Let your company of good success know what's going on. This strengthens your position, and you get support.

6. <u>Practice</u> your plan.

Here are some examples of setting boundaries:

• Goal: I will not drink alcohol with my classmates.

Boundary: I will go to the movies with my classmates, but I will not go to the club where they usually party and drink after the movies.

• Goal: I will not engage in teenage sex.

Boundary: I will not go on a late-night drive with the guy or girl who likes me.

• Goal: I will not cheat on my test.

Boundary: I will study hard for the test.

The idea of creating boundaries is consciously setting up ways or strategies that will help you to accomplish your goal.

In the first example, not going to the club where there is alcohol will help that person from being pressured to drink. Creating this defense works for him. Congratulations, buddy!

The person who does not want to have sex decided that he/she will not go into a car on a lonely dark road with a guy/girl because the chances of having sex is great. That is one boundary that will work. Kudos!

The person who does not want to be tempted to cheat on the test decided to study. Hello!

There are many situations that you will face as a young person, and when boundaries are in place, and a situation arises, it will be easier to prevent a pitfall. Now that I have provoked you to think about them, begin to practice setting boundaries during the next activity.

Setting boundaries before you are faced with challenges will help you to make quick and sound decisions when under pressure.

No - Pit - 4 - Us
Activity 4

Break out into two groups and have each group take either activity A or activity B.

A. Look at the nine questions that should be considered when attempting to identify potential pitfalls. Create a scenario or example for each one and discuss how to prevent that pitfall.

1. Is it a secret?

2. Do you have knowledge and details about the activity?

3. Will you be isolated?

4. Is this a risky operation?

5. Do you feel forced?

6. Do you feel restricted or controlled?

7. Are you being bribed?

8. Is the activity illegal?

9. What value or virtue is in this for me?

B. Have a discussion with your group and come up with specific boundaries to protect against the following:

1. Use of alcohol

2. Drunk driving

3. Teenage sex

4. Cheating

5. Pornography

6. Use of drugs

7. Sexting

8. Gang relations

9. Stealing

10. Murder

11. Bullying

12. Dropping out of high school

13. Any other situations you can come up with

CHAPTER EIGHT

A SURRENDERED LIFE

A. Order My Steps

"Life is a drag. Things are not going well. What a messed-up situation! I can't live like this any longer! I need help!"

When a person admits to his/her weakness, this allows God to demonstrate his power in them. Our heavenly Father does not violate our will, but when we are willing to accept His way and His help, He is ready and very capable of seeing us through our issues.

Regardless of one's age, whether a child, teenager, or adult; regardless of one's educational accomplishment, a certificate, a high school diploma, or college degree; regardless of one's job, whether a fireman, nurse, lawyer, teacher, or governor; there are times in our lives when we have to be truthful with ourselves, throw our hands up in the air and say, "God, I surrender. I need your help."

As you surrender to God, ask Him to order your steps. When you pray, ask Abba Father to show you what to do, how to do it, where to go, and where not to go. God, in His wisdom, will direct you. For example, if you ask God what you should study for a particular exam, he may have one of your classmates call you and say, "Hey, I think you should study all of chapter two." BAM! When you go in to take the test, the entire exam is on chapter two. That is one way God may work on your behalf. Just believe and trust in Him with your whole heart.

God is all-knowing, omniscient. He is everywhere at the same time, omnipresent. So if He knows everything and He is everywhere at the same time, to me, that is the best best company to have! God is the company to have. Ultimately, a surrendered life is accepting God's Son, Jesus Christ, as your Lord and Savior. John 3:16 states, "For God so loved the world, that he give his only begotten Son, that whosoever believeth in him should not perish, but have everlasting life." God loves you so much, and all He wants you to do is surrender your life to Him and allow Him to order your steps to an abundant life.

B. Finding Good Success

We all know that success is when things turn out well. A test score of 100% or winning a scholarship for college are exciting accomplishments. Good success is founded on the promises of God's Word. If God says to do what His Word says and you will have good success, then you will have good success. I am not arguing with that!

God has the plan in His Word for every situation in your life. He is your creator, and He knows your needs. To find good success, hang out and hang in there with God. He promises to keep you on course to great achievements.

> Joshua 1:8 "This book of the law shall not depart out of thy mouth; but thou shalt meditate therein day and night, that thou mayest observe to do according to all that is written therein: for then thou shalt make thy way prosperous, and then thou shalt have good success."

CONCLUSION

A. Empowered: Risen Against the Pitfalls of Life

Hooray! You made it to the conclusion. I am super proud of you! Your journey through this book of invaluable information is over, and your journey to work through what you have learned begins. Knowledge is power. Now that you have acquired much more knowledge about life, be empowered, and use the information you have acquired to your advantage.

- If you did not know, now you know that pitfalls cause some situations that make people's lives miserable.

- If you did not know, now you know how to protect yourself against the pitfalls of life.

- If you did not know, now you know what it takes to overcome peer pressure.

You now have the tools, so open your toolbox and use what you have learned to hammer, asphyxiate, and mash up anything and everything that will try to derail you from achieving your goals. If things get rough and you fall, get up and try again. Believe in yourself and set your mind to achieve. I am already excited about how the Lord will work with you as you allow Him to be Lord of your life.

B. Challenged to Take a Stand

"Those who stand for nothing fall for anything."
–Anonymous.

I dare to say that your generation will not fall into the pitfalls of life.

I dare to say that you will rise to every occasion to dismantle the plans of the devil, whose intention is to steal from you, kill you, and destroy you.

I challenge you to stand tall, and to embrace and hold on to everything that God has promised you. His promise to you is good success; so be strong and courageous and make His promises happen in your life. You are smart! You can do it! Eventually, dodging pitfalls will be "easy peasy," no sweat!

Finally, never forget, reject, or dismiss your company of good success. After all, they are committed to you. Build a great relationship with them and allow their wisdom, guidance, friendship, and love to propel you to achieve your best life.

Are you ready? Are you set? Okay! Now go and take the ultimate challenge: *No - Pit - 4 - Us!*

C. Prayer for the Rising Generation

Heavenly Father, I come to you in the name of your Son, Jesus Christ. Dear Lord, I bring every teen that has read this book before your throne, and I pray that what they have read would move deeply into their hearts, and they would develop an unstoppable zeal to circumvent the traps that the enemy has set for them.

Father, I pray that this mighty army of youths will acknowledge you as their creator, sustainer, provider, guide, strength, wisdom, and hope. Father, I pray that they will seek first the Kingdom of God and your righteousness so that all good things will be added unto them.

It is my prayer, Abba Father, that they would learn about you and embrace your wisdom to make the best decisions in life.

Lord Jesus, the enemy of their souls so wants them to be engulfed by pitfalls, so I pray that you will strengthen them to resist the temptations of the devil; cover them with your precious blood so that the enemy would have no place in their lives, and let your anointing flow over them so that they will be able to withstand, and having done all, to stand (Ephesians 6:13).

Like Ephesians 6, may this generation be strong in the Lord and in the power of His might. May they put on the full armor of God so that they will be able to stand against the devil's schemes. I pray that they will put on the full armor of God so that when the day of evil comes, they will be able to stand their ground.

Father, many of them may have already fallen into a pit of trouble. But like Joseph, who was rescued after his brothers threw him into a pit, Father, I pray that you will send a company of good success to rescue these young people from a place of despair to a place of hope, healing, and restoration.

Strengthen them to resist negative peer pressure and preserve them from danger and destruction.

May they honor and serve you all the days of their lives.

Bless this rising generation who has taken the challenge:
No - Pit - 4 - Us. In Jesus's name, I pray, Amen!

REFERENCES

1. Oxford University Press. "Pitfall." Oxford Dictionaries | English, Oxford Dictionaries, 2019, en.oxforddictionaries. com/pitfall.

2. "Spirit, Soul and Body, Your Greatest Trouble by Dr. Myles Munroe." YouTube, 5 Nov. 2018, www.youtube.com/ watch?v=D_7mOXjRvWI.

3. "Peer Pressure." Merriam-Webster, 2019, www.merriam-webster.com/dictionary/peer%20pressure.

4. "Understanding the Teen Brain." Understanding the Teen Brain - Health Encyclopedia - University of Rochester Medical Center, 2019, www.urmc.rochester.edu/ encyclopedia.

5. WebMD, LLC. "How Alcohol Affects Your Body." WebMD, 2017, www.webmd.com/mental-health/addiction/ss/ slideshow-alcohol-body-effects.

6. CBHSQ Report. "CDC - Fact Sheets-Underage Drinking - Alcohol." Centers for Disease Control and Prevention, 16 May 2017, www.cdc.gov/alcohol/fact-sheets/underage-drinking. htm.

7. CDC, Alcohol and Public Health. "Fact Sheet – Underage Drinking." Centers for Disease Control and Prevention, 2 August 2018. https://www.cdc.gov/alcohol/fact-sheets/

underage-drinking.htm.

U.S. Department of Health and Human Services. The Surgeon General's Call to Action to Prevent and Reduce Underage Drinking. Rockville, MD: U.S. Department of Health and Human Services; 2007.

Bonnie, R.J. and O'Connell, M.E., editors. Reducing Underage Drinking: A Collective Responsibility. National Research Council and Institute of Medicine, Committee on Developing a Strategy to Reduce and Prevent Underage Drinking. Division of Behavioral and Social Sciences and Education. Washington, DC: The National Academies Press, 2004. Miller, J.W., Naimi, T.S., Brewer, R.D., Jones, S.E. Binge drinking and associated health risk behaviors among high school students. Pediatrics 119 (2007):76–85.

8. Cambridge English Dictionary. "Confidence." Cambridge Dictionary, 2019, dictionary.cambridge.org/dictionary/english/confidence.

9. Oxford University Press. "Boundary." Oxford Dictionaries - English, Oxford Dictionaries, 2019, en.oxforddictionaries.com/definition/boundary.

www.ingramcontent.com/pod-product-compliance
Lightning Source LLC
Chambersburg PA
CBHW070134100426
42744CB00009B/1828